THE BOC
THE BREAST

for Rus.
with Every blessing.

DANA Dana
LITTLEPAGE SMITH

Published by Cinnamon Press
Meirion House,
Glan yr afon,
Tanygrisiau
Blaenau Ffestiniog,
Gwynedd, LL41 3SU
www.cinnamonpress.com

ISBN: 978-1-910836-59-0

British Library Cataloguing in Publication Data. A CIP record for this book can be obtained from the British Library.

Designed and typeset in Palatino by Cinnamon Press.
Cover design by Jan Fortune.
Printed in Poland

Cinnamon Press is represented in the UK by Inpress Ltd and in Wales by the Welsh Books Council

Acknowledgements

With thanks to Drue Heinz and the Hawthornden Fellowship which allowed me to refine these poems and in gratitude for those who work at Hawthornden castle making it a refuge for so many writers.

Contents

When remedies are past, the griefs are ended.
Othello I:3

To *the National Health Service and to all women and men who work for it.*
And to Sarah Delfont and the Force Cancer Charity and the marvellous souls there who make the treatment process so much lighter with their love.

The Book of the Breast

On Overhearing A Conversation Between My Breasts

Not *why me* but why *not* me?
Wise breast, I see you know
the ways of the world. Life's sweet
but-for-grace-of— I-go
                                        wanderings—
Its roads,
its wonders: holt and heath.
Its bruise and bloom,
its hapless luck.
Heart's ease
& dog toothed violet.

My Breast And I Visit Imhotep, Egypt, 3000 BC

He gives sons to the childless.
He touches the lame,
the listless. Dispenses
thyme for pain.
His temple outside
Memphis is busy
with human bustle.
He gives balsam apple,
and onions for the breathless.
Bees halo the wounds
he smears with honey.
One touch with a crumb
of burning frankincense
and a girl stops bleeding.
This scorpion in my breast
needs his knife. Then balm
of juniper, mustard seeds, aloe.
Yet when he touches,
my writhing stone
his hand retreats.
For you I can do nothing, he says
then feeds the wind with poppies.

Hope

Things out of hope are compas't oft' with vent'ring
Venus and Adonis, William Shakespeare

Hopeless hope—without horizons.
Hope's coffers jammed,
then just as quickly—emptied.
Hope's lost self-repairing gene.
Hope's scaffold towering.

Hopeful CD 47 tumor fighting
machine. Triple negative hope—
for everything. Hope's nothing
glands secreting sweat and scent.

Hope's areola souring.
Flower of hope, sickening.
Bilious hope, neoplasming.
We're hopeful, right? Just venturing.

On the Need To Smash Some Earthenware Pottery

I could have chosen a plain white bowl,
mass produced, made in China.
Or a chipped plate. Charity shop bargain.
But I was holding this Spanish plate
twenty year companion at breakfast,
lunch and dinner. It was a blue swirling cosmos.
White flames were brightly fired into clay.
I thought about it. I might have fetched a bowl
that was nothing. (The surgeon explained
how she would cut round the aureole,
with any luck lift the tumour, stitch me up—)
so I lifted the bowl, listening to the moment's
stern requirement: a letting go of something
so dear, daily touched—so taken for granted.

For Lincoln And Churchill: Breast Cancer Survivors

Abe and Winston's biopsies are
deleted from history's pages.
Surreal. Ask anyone
how strangely these things go
diagnosed, flesh tendered,
cut. Lymph nodes flame—
a storm of sour-sweet days
our lives, lovely and receding.

Breast Tutor

Once upon a time,
before this busy
hospital life, I tutored
an excluded child,
living rough.
He saw Love deeply
double breasted.

His desperate hand fumble—
in mid-air was something
I never reported.
Who knew the look
of one delinquent,
de-tumored B-cup
breast might be
a moment's consolation.

On Bathing A Dying Woman In Haiti

I remember water-ways of urine,
dark channels cut into concrete.
Better the packed earth outside,
I thought, better the sun.
But the nuns who'd worked here forever
said no, the dark was enough.
They gave me a rag, and a bucket.
They told me to ask for fresh ones
when I moved to another woman.
Told me to start where I was.
Right there, with this chicken thin
woman, flighty but now grounded,
close to the end, no family,
just me, a girl afraid of her own shadow.

She lifted one breast for me to bathe.
Took out tiny bones and a locket,
tobacco twisted in paper. Showed me her charm
for Papa Legbe, God of crossroads.
He'd ridden her close in life, would ride
her into death. I rinsed the flannel
with a rind of soap, tucked her God back
into her one place of safety, treasure-hold,
shrunken teat, old milk-less kingdom.

Before Surgery: My Breasts And I Consider Heraclitus, Rivers

It's been decided, a breast can flow.
The same breast, sliced can be crossed twice,
can be divided against itself, left standing.
A breast in the hand is decidedly worth two
in the bush—so says my surgeon. A cut breast
remembers the knife. (Wm Blake.) A breast
is a breast is a breast—says Gertrude Stein.
The electric double breasted Whitman knew
a breast contains multitudes: Yonkers, Ellis Island.
This morning I will cross over my breast's bloody
isthmus, minus one sliver. If lucky, I will cross
and re-cross time's bright and priceless river.

Vincent van Gogh Asks To Paint My Breasts

This sorrow shall never pass, I wrote that once,
but now I know how *everything* passes
so let us see your breasts in that light,
dark as lemons.

He has lit a small fire, whether or not anyone comes—
Or I might paint them as oranges.
Or olives, the green fruit of possibility.

No! he corrects himself, *Since night*
has many colours I shall paint your breasts
as brightness unperceived, as black *as olives.*

He picks up brushes. Seven plates of oil wait.
Lemon heaped near cobalt, lime seeps into violet.
Disrobing, I ask, 'What did you do when the terror came?'

The ravens bore down on me.
Burning fields of wheat anointed me.
I accepted all creation: its withered shoes, potatoes.

Your breast: touch its scar seam.
Let us look closely at the halved, bruised
a periwinkle green about to turn—golden.

Common Prayer, Chemo Soup

Monday:
The eel pot of my gut is a snake tangle.
I heave a stream down river.

Tuesday:
My senses veer. I spew berry bright,
rough scat—confuse the foxes.

Wednesday:
I make nothing, not even a piffling wind.
The gnats take no notice.

Thursday:
Forgotten.

Friday:
My skin is shiver-sauna tingling. Blizzard
sweat. Hood up, shirt off. Lightning quick. Heat demented.

Saturday:
My husband boils me nettle leaf. Life's emetic:
rid yourself of the unnecessary. Or wait until the world does it for you.

Sunday:
Skin flames awake. A surviving friend leaves me quail eggs.
Wild garlic. Which I can draw even if I cannot eat.

The robbed that smile steal something from the thief

Othello I.3, William Shakespeare

We guess at grief.
Children? Childless?
We cast sidelong glances
across waiting rooms.
One woman's always smiling.

How goes it? I ask,
meaning the burns,
the constipation, the stew
of un-sleep, the moments
brimming in between—

& she sings, *Magic*!
As if she's glanced
some royal blue,
the bib of a blue-tit
in a secret glen off Oncology.

Magic! she says to the room—
As if one might give into it.
See a flash of woodpecker
as the cherry tree flexes
& wakes itself in blossom.

Wandering Down The Halls Of Chemistry

My oncologist inhabits the beyond of sleep.
She sips knowledge lightly, her proboscis
tapped into the vein of ripe poisons. Perhaps

she would prefer flowers, would rather bleed aloes
and heal-alls into her patients, lemon balm, balsam,
lavender oil, anointing? But we are the razed heads

of her chemical garden. Stitched children, we storm
her nights and days where she dreams us alive:
a patch of pale tubers, unruly rhizomes, newly greened horizons.

Denial Is The Dog

A radiographer asks if I'm in denial about my cancer

Denial is the dog that drops
its pongy ball between my knees.
Ball? What ball? I say to the dog.

Then I toss it over the blood black beech
through the cloudless clouds
with their invisibly deep silver linings.

And the ball bounces back.
But I ignore it. Quickly mutating
ball—histology grade three.

Chemicals scream through veins.
The ball, where is the ball?
Deep in the long grass.

Nine months on, the hairless dog
is exhausted. My lymph nodes
have lost the ball.

Here dog. I'll throw you my life.
Legless, you can leap.
Together we will find it.

My Breasts Learn To Radiate

A slug of radiation, snugly needled,
fingers its way from nipple to armpit.
The nurse says massage it,
wing your arm so that it will travel.
Cobalt x-ray plates track them.
Less radiation than a flight to Tanzania,
my surgeon says, picking up my hot bullet.
At night I sizzle. Heat's panther
shuffles round our bed--
Snuffling shudder. Our room's
a heartbeat. I hear the roar
of blood vessels in my head—
My husband's? More radiation.
This cat leaps from me, frantic.
Heart's thump and wheeze—
Could be therapeutic.

Meadowsweet

The doctor never said to me,
Go home. Give your life some order.
No, the milkmaid came. Milkmaid,
though she was fifty-three,
steady as a plough horse.
A mane of wildflowers
down her back. She walked
in perfect balance,
a well-topped bucket hung
from each hand. In one, milk frothed,
flowered with wild honey.
In the other, a pool of wild bees
hummed.
She laughed, milk-maid,
milk-crone, her pace steady.
She tipped one bucket out,
unafraid of the winged stream.
I felt a slip of shackles.

Good, she said
and laughed.
Her dense breasts,
or what was left of them,
her canny smile,
just showing.

Admitting The Light

My breast is knifed
by unseen light.
An iris aperture lets it fly.
Week on week.
Time slides.
The speed of light
bends closer.
I lie like meat,
Fountains of electrons
slalom course, slide
Ricochet
off tungsten.

Life seeding death,
death magnetised by life.

My Breasts And I Regard The First Bloom Of Nectarine

Dried daubs of red
dead, tight bunched tomatoes,
hang on the vine
after long winter.

Beneath them mint greens.
Thyme survives much rain.
Prunus Persica. Early gem
manages one bud.
Winds change.

My Breasts And I Discourse With Fanny Burney

Fanny Burney was operated on for breast cancer by Napoleon's surgeon without anaesthetic.

Trivial, it seems, a little thing—
the grand business not yet over

Radioactive boosts to bed of breast.
Light bombarding.

My ovaries stewed, chemically.
Sun-flares flush from cheek to nipple.

I walked till I was nearly stupid.
The room entered by seven men in black.

CCTV, means they see if I move a millimetre.
And if I twitch? We scream.

A bedstead was placed in the middle of the room.
I had been told an armchair would suffice.

Through cambric I saw him draw a straight line,
cross it, trace a circle. The WHOLE to be taken off.

Cutting against the grain, I began to scream
the knife tackling against breast bone...

So indescribably sensitive was the spot—
I called out twice before I fainted, Tell me! Tell me!

When I ask for survival rates,
the new doctor asks, 'Do you want me to say?

Can I say?'—*I was sick...*
disordered by a single question.

I Walk With An Old Man

This wheezing old man walks with a wall at his side,
I wait. Until the wall ends.
Then I offer myself

His taxi is late. We stand
our breaths meet as
we talk about the Romans,

beautiful women he has loved,
the North. Your wife? I ask,
She died...

and then he says a word
I can't make out. I ask him
to repeat it. Three times.

I get it, the fourth time
She died, elegantly.
I sweat, his dribble shines.

My Breasts And I Going Flying In An Apache Over The Hindu Kush

Happy dayz. She says & high fives me.
It's all techies and dark info.
My breasts are sweating, wet.

War will be 'surgical', 'frictionless'.
Is it the altitude?
My breasts have started to bleed.

I have to leave. In the loos,
my breasts are red as the graffiti
the militarisation of America

will bring America to its knees. 'Dana!'
someone's calling, 'Our exercise is not to kill,
just persuade.'

Drones & satellites....
Now the gunner looks at me:
Your boobs are sad lady.

He paints a *sad face*
with my bosom
blood in the dirt.

My breasts have known
their knives.
My bloody breasts.

My scarred & healing flesh.
The same as that kid's.
His sisters' and his mother's.

My Breasts And I Consider Queen Elizabeth I

She never saw herself after she became old in a true glass; they painted her and sometymes would vermillion her nose.

Ben Jonson in conversation with Drummond of Hawthornden

Agued membrane
of mortality,
I give you leave.
Armies of damage
each day
unseen agencies.
Mirror mirroring.
Scarred necropolis.
Sweet mutability.
This holy grail, my body.

This holy grail,
my body
sweet mutability
necropolis of scars.
Mirror mirroring.
Unseen agencies.
Armies of damage
daily, *aged, agued.*
Mortality, I do not want
to give you leave.

On The Last Day Of Treatment, The Teacher Places A Sword In My Hands

Into my hands she places this sword
of smelted steel, double helixed iron,
iron flayed and forged in the fire,

sword that can cut a woman
down from her death.
Sword that skins the fat off inattention.

Sword I've ill-used.
Double-helixed, commonplace—
My only.

A Wise Man Teaches About Mutating Bodies

He receives what I think is a telescope in the mail—
No, he corrects me.

It is his catheter. A ninety year old body
needs a re-think. His spine teaches him new lessons.

This going downhill is all uphill work.
He walks the halls of night, gently smiling.

My Breasts And I Consider A Girl Who Only Walked Backwards

Uphill's hardest—easier shoeless.
Not looking over her shoulder.
Blind to the world of what was coming.

Shoulders blades become velvet,
moth's antennae,
alert to every wind.

Corridors mean lethal comers.
Steps are a circus
of unreal expectations.

Never puts her best foot
forward. Hawk-eyed
tenses to every shadow.

Survival takes strange
forms them quietly
hoists them on us.

Study Of A Breast

Bathing next to a girl of sixteen
in the public showers
her breast is beautiful, wet,
ten inches away.

My breasts have suffered
their blades, the world
soul went on dreaming
its milk flesh embodied.

My handful of flesh
dense as the star
point of galaxies
has fallen slightly inward.

Less than a universe away
a breast is en-caved
in its sky of galactic streams,
light's curtains.

A God's first fumblings:
his handful of flesh,
as he suckles his mother's
olive skinned cream.

A Surviving Friend Takes Me Cliff-walking

There's no controlling this.
Needs must:
walk on your hands
and knees.
The pre-arranged
is nothing to rely on.
Even when the path
seems gravity
defying,
cling to the dust
that bathes your body.

My Breasts And I Consider The Yellow Pimpernel, Wood Sorrel

I lie down in the cemetery
for a short sweet sleep
in the longhouse of August.
The stun-gun of chemistry
has slain me. Cow parsley
laces sky. A crucifix
of limber green,
loose strife flowering.
Some people stop,
ask if they can help.

'No thanks, I'm fine...
Just introducing myself
to the neighbours:
the speedwell and the daisies.'

My Breasts And I Prepare For A Talk On The Nature Of Light

Once when I was a teacher, a child revealed to me that light
can travel a billion years to find us. She really wanted me to get that—
I was too tired, too rushed. Blindly blooming in cancer's hothouse.

Day after day, she'd say, *When you see light you touch it.*
So when, wheeled out of the op, I *see* this old woman who has lost
her mind and minds it. I *see* her. Alone at her hospital crossroads,

stunned as Oedipus after his great debacle. I sit up on the gurney
and smile at her. Ask to be parked so I may take her hand.
Her mewling screams retreat to a sing-song glug gurgle chortle.

I look long at her, holding her unquiet gaze, I tell her
how once when I was a teacher, a child taught me that
light travels billions of years to find us. *When you see light you touch it.*

On Bidding Cancer Adieu

Over the ridge one vulture drifts,
out-rider of my dreams,
a year's brief hospital-happenings
—gone on a thermal. My tea-spoon-

worth of stem cells signed-off
for research are lost en-route
to California. Pitch-up in Transylvania.
Life's like that. Haired, wolf-strange.

My wilding breasts lope off
through new hinterlands.
Uncountable days of bliss,
and sorrow, blood,
piss and sweet marrow.

www.ingramcontent.com/pod-product-compliance
Ingram Content Group UK Ltd.
Pitfield, Milton Keynes, MK11 3LW, UK
UKHW042124120325
456182UK00002B/162

* 9 7 8 1 9 1 0 8 3 6 5 9 0 *